THE 17 BUSINESS LESSONS Insights from Christo Wiese

A Masterclass in Entrepreneurship by South African Retail Mogul

Dave Njogu

Published by Babazuri Creative Firm
x.com/bcreativefirm[1]

---

1. http://x.com/bcreativefirm

While every precaution has been taken in the preparation of this book, the publisher assumes no responsibility for errors or omissions, or for damages resulting from the use of the information contained herein.

THE 17 BUSINESS LESSONS INSIGHTS FROM CHRISTO WIESE

First edition. July 12, 2024.

ISBN: 979-8227015624

Written by Dave Njogu.

Also by Dave Njogu

101 Common Questions Answered
Mastering Business English Q&A

Standalone
The Healing Harvest: Organic Farming 101
Unlock Your Authorial Potential: The Ultimate Guide to
Crafting and Selling eBooks Using ChatGPT and Draft2digit
Herbs and Spices: Nature's Remedies for Health and Wellness
Grit and Growth: Unleashing Mental Toughness for Small
Business Success
Design Mastery: Principles of Page Layout and Typography
for Beginners
The Quantity Advantage: Achieving Excellence Through
Abundance
THE 17 BUSINESS LESSONS Insights from Christo Wiese

Table of Contents

To Christo Wiese,

Your profound insights and invaluable lessons have inspired this work. This book is a tribute to your remarkable journey and the wisdom you've shared, which will guide and motivate entrepreneurs around the world.

And to all aspiring business leaders,

May these lessons serve as a guiding light on your path to success, reminding you that with determination, positivity, and resilience, you can achieve your dreams.

With sincere appreciation,

Dave Njogu

Preface

I ntroduction to the Purpose of the Book

The journey of entrepreneurship is a path filled with countless challenges, opportunities, successes, and setbacks. For many aspiring businesspeople, the path to success can seem elusive and daunting. This book aims to demystify the process by sharing the invaluable insights of one of South Africa's most successful retail businessmen, Christo Wiese. Through his hard-earned lessons, we aim to provide a roadmap for anyone looking to embark on or navigate their entrepreneurial journey.

The Inspiration Behind the Book

The idea for this book was sparked by a chance encounter with a YouTube video. While browsing through videos about entrepreneurs, I stumbled upon an interview titled, ***"In this video, I sit down with my father, South African retail businessman Christo Wiese, for a masterclass in entrepreneurship and business. He shares 17 priceless and hard-earned business lessons that have helped guide his path to success and his ability to overcome setbacks." – Clare Wiese-Wentzel***. Intrigued, I decided to download the video and watch it offline.

As I watched Clare Wiese-Wentzel interview her father, I was struck by the depth of wisdom and practical advice he shared. The lessons were not just theoretical; they were grounded in real-world experience, reflecting both the triumphs and tribulations of a long and distinguished career. It became clear to me that these insights could benefit a wider audience if presented in a structured and accessible format. This realization led to the decision to write this book.

Amplifying the Message

The primary objective of this book is to amplify Christo Wiese's message so that it is easy to learn, understand, and most importantly, apply in our business careers. The 17 business lessons shared by Wiese cover a broad spectrum of topics essential for entrepreneurial success, from developing a positive mindset to managing debt, from the importance of interpersonal skills to understanding the power of compound interest.

By distilling these lessons into concise chapters, each with practical takeaways, I hope to make the wisdom of Christo Wiese accessible to a global audience. Each chapter is designed to provide actionable insights that readers can implement immediately in their business endeavors.

THE IMPORTANCE OF CHRISTO Wiese's Business Philosophy

Christo Wiese's business philosophy is grounded in pragmatism, resilience, and an unwavering belief in the potential of the individual. His approach to business emphasizes the importance of a positive attitude, ethical conduct, and the relentless pursuit of excellence. His lessons are not just about making money but about building a sustainable and fulfilling business career.

Wiese's insights on dealing with setbacks, making difficult decisions, and maintaining interpersonal relationships are particularly valuable in today's fast-paced and often unpredictable business environment. His emphasis on continuous learning, adaptability, and humility serves as a reminder that success is not a destination but a journey.

By sharing these lessons, we aim to inspire and equip the next generation of entrepreneurs with the tools they need to succeed. Whether you are just starting out or looking to take your business to the next level, the wisdom of Christo Wiese can provide the guidance and inspiration you need to achieve your goals.

In closing, I hope that this book will serve as a beacon of knowledge and inspiration for all who read it. May the lessons within empower you to navigate the challenges of entrepreneurship with confidence and resilience, and may they guide you to success in your business endeavors.

Chapter 1: Brief Biography of Christo Wiese

Early Life

Childhood and Family Background in South Africa
Christoffel Wiese, commonly known as Christo Wiese, was born on September 10, 1941, in Upington, a small town in the Northern Cape province of South Africa. Growing up in a modest, rural environment, Wiese was deeply influenced by his family's values of **hard work**, **integrity**, and **perseverance**. His father, a successful businessman, instilled in him the importance of dedication and resilience from an early age.

The Wiese family valued education and self-improvement, setting the foundation for Christo's future endeavors. This nurturing environment, combined with the challenges of growing up in a remote part of South Africa, shaped Wiese's character and prepared him for the ups and downs of the business world.

Education and Early Influences

CHRISTO WIESE ATTENDED Paarl Boys' High School, a prestigious institution known for its academic rigor and emphasis on discipline. His time at Paarl Boys' High was pivotal, as it exposed him to diverse ideas and fostered a sense of ambition.

After high school, Wiese pursued a Bachelor of Arts degree at Stellenbosch University, where he majored in Law. His legal studies provided him with critical thinking skills and a strong foundation in logic and reasoning, which would prove invaluable in his business career. During his university years, Wiese was influenced by a variety of thinkers and business leaders, further shaping his entrepreneurial mindset.

Career Beginnings

INITIAL VENTURES AND Early Career Milestones

After completing his education, Christo Wiese began his career in the legal profession, practicing as an attorney. However, his entrepreneurial spirit soon led him to seek opportunities beyond the confines of law. Wiese's first major business venture was with Pep Stores, a retail company that would later become a cornerstone of his business empire.

Wiese joined Pep Stores in the 1960s, a time when the company was still in its infancy. He quickly recognized the potential for growth in the retail sector, particularly in providing affordable clothing and goods to lower-income consumers. His strategic vision and innovative approach helped Pep Stores expand rapidly, setting the stage for Wiese's future successes.

Key Challenges and How He Overcame Them

Wiese faced numerous challenges in the early stages of his career. The South African economy was volatile, and the retail sector was highly competitive. Additionally, operating in a country marked by political and social unrest required navigating complex regulatory and societal issues.

Despite these obstacles, Wiese's determination and strategic acumen allowed him to overcome setbacks. He focused on building a strong management team, streamlining operations, and leveraging economies of scale. His ability to adapt to changing market conditions and his unwavering commitment to his vision were key factors in his early success.

Rise to Prominence

EXPANSION INTO RETAIL and Other Industries

Christo Wiese's major breakthrough came with the rapid expansion of Pep Stores, which eventually became Pepkor, a retail conglomerate with a diverse portfolio of brands. Under his leadership, Pepkor grew from a small chain of stores into a dominant force in the South African retail market, known for its **affordable products and extensive reach.**

Wiese didn't limit himself to retail; he ventured into various other industries, including real estate, financial services, and investments. His acquisition of Shoprite, a leading supermarket chain, marked a significant milestone. Shoprite expanded under Wiese's guidance to become the largest food retailer in Africa, known for its aggressive pricing and extensive store network.

Major Successes and Acquisitions

Some of Christo Wiese's notable successes include:

- **Pepkor**: Transformed from a small retail chain into a multinational retail giant.

- **Shoprite**: Expanded to over 15 countries in Africa, serving millions of customers with a wide range of products.

- **Brait SE**: Wiese's investment firm, which made significant investments in various sectors, including healthcare and consumer goods.

- **Steinhoff International**: Although this investment faced significant challenges later, it was initially part of Wiese's strategy to diversify and expand his business interests globally.

Philosophical Framework

WIESE'S CORE BELIEFS and Values That Guided His Career

Throughout his career, Christo Wiese adhered to a set of core beliefs and values that guided his decision-making and leadership style. These include:

- **Resilience** : Wiese firmly believed in the importance of perseverance, especially in the face of adversity. He often emphasized that setbacks are a natural part of any business journey and that one's ability to recover and learn from them defines true success.

- **Integrity**: Ethical conduct and transparency were central to Wiese's business philosophy. He maintained that long-term success could only be achieved by building trust with customers, employees, and stakeholders.

- **Innovation**: Wiese valued creativity and the willingness to take calculated risks. He encouraged his teams to think outside the box and continuously seek new opportunities for growth and improvement.

- **Empathy and Respect**: Understanding and respecting people was a fundamental aspect of Wiese's leadership. He believed that treating employees and partners with dignity and compassion was essential for fostering a positive and productive work environment.

- **Optimism**: Incurable optimism was perhaps the most defining characteristic of Wiese's outlook on life and business. He consistently focused on the potential for success and the opportunities that lay ahead, regardless of the challenges.

Christo Wiese's remarkable journey from a small-town boy to a leading figure in the global business community is a testimony to his vision, hard work, and unwavering commitment to his principles.

His story serves as an inspiration to aspiring entrepreneurs, illustrating that with the right mindset and determination, success is within reach for anyone willing to pursue it passionately.

Chapter 2: The Biggest Business Lesson

No Magic to Success

Understanding That Successful Businesspeople Are Not Magical

One of the most profound lessons that Christo Wiese emphasizes is the notion that there is **no magic to becoming a successful businessperson.** This insight is rooted in his own journey and observations over decades in the business world. Wiese insists that **successful individuals are not endowed with supernatural abilities or secret formulas.** Instead, they are ordinary people who have harnessed certain principles and practices to achieve their goals.

In many ways, this perspective demystifies the path to success. It challenges the common belief that only a select few, possessing extraordinary talents or intelligence, can reach the pinnacles of business. Wiese's message is empowering: **success is accessible to anyone who is willing to work for it.**

Developing a Philosophical Framework

Wiese's approach to business is deeply influenced by his personal philosophical framework, which consists of five core elements: faith, positivity, hard work, enthusiasm, and compassion.

(i) Faith:

Faith, for Wiese, is not only a religious concept but also a belief in oneself and one's vision. This faith provides the resilience needed to navigate the inevitable challenges and setbacks in business. It instills a sense of purpose and direction, helping entrepreneurs stay committed to their goals even when the path forward seems uncertain.

(ii) Positivity:

Positivity is another cornerstone of Wiese's philosophy. He firmly believes that a positive attitude can transform obstacles into opportunities. This optimistic outlook not only boosts morale but also fosters a productive and innovative work environment. **By focusing on what can be achieved rather than what could go wrong, positive thinking energizes individuals and teams, driving them towards their objectives.**

(iii) Hard Work:

Hard work is a non-negotiable aspect of success in Wiese's view. He underscores the importance of diligence and perseverance. Success, according to Wiese, is often a result of sustained effort and a relentless pursuit of excellence. **Hard work involves not just putting in long hours but also striving for continuous improvement and being willing to go the extra mile.**

(iv) Enthusiasm:

Enthusiasm is the fuel that keeps the entrepreneurial spirit alive. Wiese believes that passion for one's work is crucial. This enthusiasm is infectious; it motivates others and creates a dynamic, energetic workplace. When leaders are genuinely excited about their vision and goals, it inspires their teams to share in that excitement and work collectively towards success.

(v) Compassion

Compassion, though often overlooked in the business world, is a vital component of Wiese's philosophy. Treating people with kindness and respect builds a loyal and motivated workforce. **Compassionate leadership involves understanding and addressing the needs and aspirations of employees, customers, and partners**. It fosters a culture of trust and collaboration, which is essential for long-term success.

Encouraging Belief That Anybody Can Make It

Christo Wiese's message is ultimately one of hope and inclusivity. He encourages the belief that **anybody, regardless of their background or circumstances, can achieve success. This belief is not merely motivational rhetoric but is grounded** in Wiese's own experiences and observations.

Throughout his career, Wiese has seen countless examples of individuals who, through determination and adherence to these principles, have transformed their lives and businesses. He argues that **the primary barriers to success are often self-imposed: fear of failure, lack of self-belief, and unwillingness to take risks.**

By adopting a philosophical framework of faith, positivity, hard work, enthusiasm, and compassion, aspiring entrepreneurs can equip themselves with the tools needed to succeed. Wiese's teachings emphasize that success is a journey marked by continuous learning and growth. It is about developing the right mindset and habits that enable one to navigate the complexities of the business world effectively.

*In In Summary, the biggest business lesson that Christo Wiese offers is both simple and profound: there is no magic to success. It is the result of a thoughtful, disciplined approach grounded in universal principles. By embracing this lesson, **anyone can embark on a path to success, driven by faith, positivity, hard work, enthusiasm, and compassion.** This lesson serves as a beacon of hope for all who aspire to achieve their dreams in the business world.*

Chapter 3: What You Need to Accept

Business Ups and Downs

Accepting the Inevitable Ups and Downs of a Business Career

In the journey of entrepreneurship, one of the first and most crucial lessons is accepting that business, much like life, is fraught with ups and downs. Christo Wiese emphasizes that understanding and embracing this reality is vital for anyone looking to build a successful career in business. The path to success is rarely a straight line; it is often marked by peaks of triumph and valleys of challenges.

Wiese's own career is a testimony to this truth. He has experienced both remarkable successes and significant setbacks, each contributing to his growth and resilience as a business leader. Accepting the fluctuations of a business career means preparing oneself mentally and emotionally for the highs and lows. It involves cultivating a mindset that remains steady in the face of adversity and does not become complacent during prosperous times.

Measuring Success by How You Handle Setbacks

For Wiese, true success is not merely about reaching the top but is defined by how one handles setbacks along the way. **Setbacks are inevitable, but they are also opportunities for learning and growth.** Wiese believes that resilience is a key attribute of successful entrepreneurs. It is the ability to bounce back from failures, learn from mistakes, and continue moving forward to big success.

Wiese's perspective is that **setbacks are not roadblocks but rather stepping stones.** Each challenge presents an opportunity to refine strategies, improve processes, and strengthen resolve. This mindset shift—from seeing setbacks as failures to viewing them as integral parts of the journey—can transform how one experiences and navigates the business world.

Handling setbacks effectively requires a combination of patience, adaptability, and a proactive approach. Wiese advises entrepreneurs to remain calm and composed when faced with difficulties. It is important to analyze what went wrong, understand the underlying causes, and implement corrective measures. By doing so, setbacks become valuable lessons that contribute to long-term success.

Importance of Counting Blessings and Not Giving Up

One of the most powerful tools for maintaining resilience in the face of business challenges is the practice of counting blessings. Wiese stresses the **importance of gratitude** as a foundational principle. In times of adversity, focusing on the positives—such as personal health, supportive relationships, and previous achievements—can provide much-needed perspective and encouragement.

THE 17 BUSINESS LESSONS INSIGHTS FROM CHRISTO WIESE

Gratitude helps to shift the focus from what is going wrong to what is still good and working well. This positive outlook can foster a sense of hope and motivation, even during the toughest times. Wiese's advice is to regularly reflect on and appreciate the small and large blessings in life and business. This practice not only boosts morale but also reinforces a mindset of abundance and possibility.

Alongside gratitude, perseverance is crucial. Wiese's mantra is simple: **do not give up**. The business landscape is competitive and ever-changing, and those who succeed are often the ones who persist when others might quit. This tenacity involves a firm belief in oneself and one's vision, even when external circumstances are challenging.

Wiese's own story is filled with instances where his refusal to give up led to eventual success. He faced numerous setbacks, including financial difficulties, market downturns, and strategic missteps. Yet, his unwavering commitment to his goals and his ability to stay the course enabled him to overcome these hurdles and achieve remarkable success.

In summary, what you need to accept in a business career is the inevitability of ups and downs. Success is not solely measured by achievements but by how you navigate and learn from setbacks. Embracing a mindset of resilience, practicing gratitude, and maintaining perseverance are key to enduring and thriving in the business world. Christo Wiese's journey exemplifies these principles, offering valuable insights for aspiring entrepreneurs who are ready to face the challenges of their own paths to success.

Chapter 4:
Interpersonal Skills

Human Interaction

Treating People with Respect and Dignity

At the core of Christo Wiese's business philosophy is the principle of treating people with respect and dignity. Whether dealing with employees, partners, customers, or competitors, Wiese believes that **every interaction should be grounded in mutual respect.** This approach is not only ethically sound but also fosters a positive and productive business environment.

Respecting others involves recognizing their inherent worth and valuing their contributions. It means listening to their ideas, acknowledging their efforts, and treating them fairly. Wiese emphasizes that showing respect is not just about politeness; it is about genuinely appreciating the human element in every business interaction. This principle extends to all levels of an organization, from top executives to frontline employees.

Dignity, on the other hand, is about ensuring that people feel valued and appreciated. Wiese believes that maintaining the dignity of others, even in challenging situations, is crucial.

This means handling conflicts and disagreements with tact and sensitivity, and always considering the impact of one's words and actions on others.

Importance of Working Well with Others and Not Making Enemies

Wiese's success can be attributed, in large part, to his ability to work well with others. He understands that **business is fundamentally about people and relationships**. Collaborating effectively with others—whether they are colleagues, partners, or stakeholders—is essential for achieving common goals.

Working well with others involves building strong, collaborative relationships based on trust and mutual respect. It requires **effective communication**, **empathy**, and a **willingness to compromise**. Wiese advises that by fostering a cooperative spirit, businesses can leverage the diverse strengths and perspectives of their teams to achieve greater success.

An important aspect of this principle is avoiding the creation of unnecessary enemies. In the competitive world of business, it can be easy to view others as adversaries. However, Wiese cautions against this mindset. Making enemies not only creates a toxic work environment but can also have long-term negative consequences. Instead, he advocates for a more inclusive approach, where competition is seen as an opportunity for mutual growth and learning.

Avoiding Burning Bridges

In line with his emphasis on positive interpersonal relationships, Wiese advises against burning bridges. The business world is interconnected, and paths often cross in unexpected ways. A relationship that seems insignificant today may prove valuable in the future. By maintaining good relationships, even when parting ways, one ensures that opportunities for collaboration and support remain open.

Avoiding burning bridges involves ending relationships on a positive note, expressing gratitude for the shared experiences, and leaving the door open for future interactions. It means handling departures—whether they are job changes, partnership dissolutions, or client terminations—with grace and professionalism.

Wiese's own career demonstrates the importance of this principle. He has navigated numerous transitions and changes in his business ventures, always striving to preserve relationships and maintain goodwill. This approach has allowed him to build a vast network of contacts and allies, which has been instrumental in his long-term success.

The Long-Term Value of Maintaining Good Relationships

Maintaining good relationships is not just about immediate benefits; it has significant long-term value. Wiese believes that strong, positive relationships form the foundation of a successful and sustainable business. **Good relationships lead to trust, loyalty, and a positive reputation—all of which are crucial for long-term success.**

Trust is a cornerstone of any successful business relationship. When people trust you, they are more likely to support your initiatives, invest in your ventures, and stand by you during challenging times. Building and maintaining trust requires consistent integrity, transparency, and reliability.

Loyalty, another key benefit of good relationships, leads to repeat business, long-term partnerships, and employee retention. **Loyal customers and clients provide a stable revenue base**, while loyal employees contribute to a cohesive and productive work environment.

A positive reputation, built on a foundation of respectful and dignified interactions, enhances a company's brand and attracts new opportunities. It can open doors to new markets, partnerships, and investments. Wiese's reputation as a fair and respectful business leader has played a significant role in his ability to attract and retain valuable relationships throughout his career.

> *In In Summary, **interpersonal skills are critical for business success**. Treating people with respect and dignity, working well with others, avoiding burning bridges, and maintaining good relationships are principles that Christo Wiese exemplifies. These skills not only create a positive and productive business environment but also provide long-term value, contributing to sustained success and growth. By cultivating these skills, aspiring entrepreneurs can build strong, resilient networks that support their business endeavors and personal growth.*

Chapter 5: Making Difficult Decisions

Embracing Uncertainty

N*o Guarantees in Life and Business*
One of the fundamental truths Christo Wiese highlights is the inherent uncertainty in life and business. **There are no guarantees, no foolproof plans, and no sure paths to success.** This uncertainty is what makes the journey both challenging and exciting. For Wiese, embracing this reality is crucial for making difficult decisions.

In the business world, unpredictability is a constant companion. Market conditions fluctuate, consumer preferences shift, and unforeseen events can disrupt even the best-laid plans. Wiese advises that understanding and accepting this lack of guarantees is the first step towards becoming an effective decision-maker. By acknowledging that uncertainty is a natural part of the process, one can approach decisions with a clearer, more resilient mindset.

Approaching Decisions Logically and Decisively
Given the unpredictable nature of business, making decisions can often feel daunting. However, Wiese believes that approaching decisions logically and decisively is key to

navigating uncertainty effectively. He emphasizes the importance of a structured and rational approach to decision-making.

1. **Gathering Information:** The first step in making any decision is to gather as much relevant information as possible. This involves researching market trends, analyzing data, consulting with experts, and understanding the potential risks and rewards. Comprehensive information provides a solid foundation for making informed choices.

2. **Weighing Options:** Once the necessary information is in hand, the next step is to evaluate the available options. This involves considering the pros and cons of each choice, assessing their feasibility, and understanding their potential impact. Wiese advises using tools such as SWOT analysis (Strengths, Weaknesses, Opportunities, Threats) to systematically evaluate options.

3. **Cutting to the Chase:** Wiese stresses the importance of cutting through the noise and getting to the heart of the matter. Business decisions can often be clouded by extraneous details and emotional biases. By focusing on the core issues and being objective, one can simplify the decision-making process and reduce the risk of paralysis by analysis.

4. **Making the Decision:** Once the options have been weighed and the core issues identified, it is crucial to make a decision and commit to it. Indecision can be detrimental, leading to missed opportunities and stagnation. Wiese believes that decisiveness is a hallmark of effective leadership. Even if a decision turns out to be less than perfect, taking action is often better than inaction.

THE 17 BUSINESS LESSONS INSIGHTS FROM CHRISTO WIESE

Accepting That Things Can Change and the Importance of Adaptability

Another critical aspect of making difficult decisions is the acceptance that circumstances can and will change. The **business environment is dynamic**, and what may seem like the right decision today could be rendered obsolete by tomorrow's developments. Wiese underscores the importance of adaptability in this context.

1. **Flexibility:** Adaptability requires a flexible mindset. This means being open to new information, willing to reassess and adjust plans, and ready to pivot when necessary. Wiese advocates for a continuous learning approach, where **one remains curious and responsive to changes** in the environment.

2. **Contingency Planning:** One way to embrace adaptability is through contingency planning. This involves anticipating possible scenarios and having backup plans in place. By considering different outcomes and preparing for them, businesses can respond more effectively to unexpected changes.

3. **Resilience:** Adaptability is also about **resilience—the ability to recover quickly from setbacks and continue moving forward.** Wiese emphasizes that setbacks are not failures but opportunities to learn and grow. Building resilience involves developing a strong support system, maintaining a positive attitude, and focusing on long-term goals despite short-term challenges.

4. **Innovation:** Finally, adaptability often requires innovation. When faced with changing circumstances, businesses must be willing to innovate—whether that means

adopting new technologies, exploring new markets, or rethinking traditional approaches. Wiese believes that a culture of innovation can help businesses stay relevant and competitive in a rapidly evolving landscape.

In Summary

Making difficult decisions is an integral part of the business journey. By embracing uncertainty, approaching decisions logically and decisively, and accepting that change is inevitable, entrepreneurs can navigate the complexities of the business world more effectively. Christo Wiese's insights provide a valuable framework for decision-making, emphasizing the importance of information, decisiveness, adaptability, and resilience. These principles not only help in making sound decisions but also in building a robust and flexible business capable of thriving amidst uncertainty.

Chapter 6: Why You Need to Be a Little Bit Crazy to Succeed

Entrepreneurial Spirit

The Need for a Bit of "Craziness" to Face the Uncertainties of Each Day

In the world of entrepreneurship, a touch of "craziness" is not just a quirky attribute; it is a necessary trait for success. Christo Wiese firmly believes that to thrive in business, one must possess a certain level of boldness and audacity that might seem unconventional or even irrational to others.

The entrepreneurial journey is inherently unpredictable and fraught with uncertainties. Every day brings new challenges, risks, and opportunities. This constant state of flux can be daunting for those who crave stability and certainty. However, for entrepreneurs like Wiese, this **unpredictability is part of the thrill and allure of business.**

Having a bit of "craziness" means being willing to step into the unknown with confidence and a sense of adventure. It involves taking risks that others might shy away from and pursuing visions that may initially seem unattainable. This daring attitude is what drives innovation and enables entrepreneurs to break new ground.

Wiese's career is a testimony to this spirit. Throughout his ventures, he has demonstrated a willingness to take bold steps, whether it was expanding into new markets, acquiring companies, or investing in unconventional projects. This willingness to embrace uncertainty and take calculated risks has been a key factor in his success.

However, this "craziness" is not about recklessness. It is about calculated boldness—assessing risks, making informed decisions, and having the courage to act on one's convictions. It requires a balance of intuition and analysis, where gut feelings are backed by solid research and strategic planning.

Maintaining Motivation Despite Potential Setbacks

The entrepreneurial spirit, infused with a bit of "craziness," is also about maintaining motivation and resilience in the face of setbacks. Setbacks are an inevitable part of the business journey. They can come in many forms—financial losses, market downturns, failed ventures, or unexpected challenges. What distinguishes successful entrepreneurs from others is their ability to stay motivated and keep moving forward despite these obstacles.

Wiese highlights the importance of a positive mindset and relentless determination. He believes that setbacks should not be seen as failures but as learning experiences. Each setback offers valuable lessons that can inform future decisions and strategies. By viewing challenges as opportunities for growth, entrepreneurs can maintain their motivation and continue to push forward.

THE 17 BUSINESS LESSONS INSIGHTS FROM CHRISTO WIESE

One way to maintain motivation is to keep a clear and compelling vision of the ultimate goal. Having a strong sense of purpose and a vivid picture of what success looks like can provide the drive needed to overcome difficulties. This vision acts as a beacon, guiding entrepreneurs through tough times and helping them stay focused on their objectives.

Another crucial aspect is **resilience—the ability to bounce back from adversity**. Resilience is built through experience, self-belief, and a supportive network. Wiese emphasizes the importance of surrounding oneself with positive, encouraging people who can provide support and perspective during challenging times. This network can include mentors, peers, family, and friends who believe in the entrepreneur's vision and offer constructive feedback and encouragement.

Moreover, maintaining motivation requires a healthy balance of optimism and realism. **While it is essential to have a positive outlook, it is equally important to be realistic about the challenges and prepare accordingly.** This balanced perspective helps entrepreneurs stay grounded while still reaching for their dreams.

Practical steps to maintain motivation include setting incremental goals, celebrating small victories, and taking care of one's physical and mental well-being. Regularly reflecting on progress, acknowledging achievements, and practicing self-care can boost morale and sustain energy levels.

In Summary

Being a little bit crazy is not about irrationality but about possessing the boldness, audacity, and resilience needed to face the uncertainties of entrepreneurship. It is about having the courage to take risks, embrace the unknown, and maintain unwavering motivation despite setbacks. Christo Wiese's insights highlight the importance of a daring entrepreneurial spirit, balanced with informed decision-making and resilience. By cultivating this mindset, aspiring entrepreneurs can navigate the unpredictable terrain of business and achieve remarkable success.

Chapter 7: Attaining vs Maintaining Wealth

Vigilance and Humility

Easier to Make Money Than to Keep It

Christo Wiese's extensive experience in the business world has led him to a profound understanding of wealth dynamics. One of his key insights is the notion that **attaining wealth is often easier than maintaining it.** Building wealth can be seen as a series of ambitious steps, often fueled by innovative ideas, strategic risks, and entrepreneurial zeal. However, once wealth is accumulated, the challenge shifts to preservation and sustainable growth.

In the initial stages of wealth creation, the focus is typically on identifying opportunities, exploiting market gaps, and executing plans with energy and determination. Entrepreneurs and business leaders are often in a proactive mode, driven by the need to establish themselves and their ventures. This phase is characterized by high levels of enthusiasm and a relentless pursuit of success.

However, once wealth is achieved, the dynamics change. The focus shifts from **aggressive growth** to **careful**

stewardship. Maintaining wealth requires a different set of skills and a heightened sense of vigilance. It involves protecting assets from market fluctuations, managing risks, and ensuring that the foundations of wealth are robust and resilient.

Staying Vigilant and Not Getting Overly Impressed with Personal Success

Wiese emphasizes the importance of vigilance in maintaining wealth. Vigilance involves constant attention to the factors that can impact wealth, both positively and negatively. It requires staying informed about market trends, economic conditions, and potential risks. This proactive approach helps in identifying threats early and taking necessary actions to mitigate them.

One of the common pitfalls for those who attain significant wealth is becoming overly impressed with their personal success. This sense of self-congratulation can lead to complacency, where the individual starts to believe that their past successes will automatically guarantee future security. Wiese warns against this mindset, as it can lead to a false sense of invulnerability.

Success can often bring with it a sense of infallibility. However, Wiese argues that it is crucial to remain humble and grounded. This humility allows individuals to stay open to learning, recognize their limitations, and seek advice when needed. It also helps in maintaining a realistic perspective on one's achievements and challenges.

Avoiding the Trap of Believing in Your Own Fairytale

Another critical aspect of maintaining wealth is avoiding the trap of believing in one's own fairytale. Success stories, especially those that involve significant wealth, can easily morph into personal myths. These myths often depict the journey as a series of flawless decisions and inevitable triumphs, overshadowing the challenges and setbacks encountered along the way.

Wiese stresses the importance of staying rooted in reality. Believing in a personal fairytale can create a disconnect between perception and reality, leading to poor decision-making. It can also result in overconfidence, where individuals start to take unnecessary risks based on their belief in their invincibility.

To avoid this trap, Wiese advises maintaining a critical and reflective approach. This involves regularly evaluating one's decisions, acknowledging mistakes, and learning from them. It also requires seeking diverse perspectives and being open to constructive criticism. By fostering an environment where honest feedback is valued, individuals can ensure that they remain grounded and make informed decisions.

Additionally, Wiese highlights the significance of ongoing education and self-improvement. The business landscape is constantly evolving, and staying updated with new knowledge and skills is essential for maintaining wealth. This continuous learning mindset helps in adapting to changes, exploring new opportunities, and staying competitive.

In Summary

Attaining wealth is often seen as the pinnacle of business success, but maintaining it requires a different set of principles and practices. Christo Wiese's insights underscore the importance of vigilance, humility, and a grounded approach to wealth management. By recognizing that it is easier to make money than to keep it, staying vigilant and humble, and avoiding the trap of believing in personal fairytales, individuals can ensure the sustainable growth and preservation of their wealth. These principles not only safeguard financial success but also promote a balanced and realistic approach to business and personal growth.

Chapter 8: The One Personality Flaw You Must Overcome

Positive Attitude

Importance of Focusing on What Can Go Right

In the area of business and personal development, Christo Wiese advocates strongly for the power of a positive attitude. He identifies it as a critical factor in overcoming challenges, achieving goals, and maintaining resilience in the face of adversity. Wiese's perspective emphasizes the transformative impact of focusing on opportunities rather than obstacles.

A positive attitude is not merely about being optimistic in the face of difficulties; it involves a deliberate mindset shift towards seeking out possibilities and solutions. Wiese encourages individuals to train their minds to look for what can go right in any situation, rather than dwelling on potential pitfalls or setbacks.

By focusing on what can go right, entrepreneurs and business leaders can foster a proactive approach to problem-solving. This mindset encourages creative thinking, innovation, and a willingness to explore new avenues for growth. It also cultivates a sense of hope and optimism among team members, fostering a supportive and forward-thinking organizational culture.

Positive Thinking as a Driver for Achievement

Wiese believes that **positive thinking is not just a passive state of mind but an active driver for achievement.** When individuals maintain a positive outlook, they are more likely to set ambitious goals, persist in the face of challenges, and seize opportunities for growth. This proactive mindset enables them to navigate setbacks with resilience and determination.

Positive thinking also influences interpersonal dynamics within teams and organizations. Leaders who embody a positive attitude inspire confidence, motivate their teams, and create an environment where innovation and collaboration thrive. This optimistic approach to leadership can have a ripple effect, boosting morale and productivity across the entire organization.

Moreover, Wiese highlights the role of positive thinking in personal well-being. A positive attitude is linked to lower stress levels, improved mental health, and enhanced overall resilience. By maintaining a constructive perspective, individuals can better manage stress, maintain focus, and sustain high levels of energy and motivation.

Practical Strategies for Cultivating a Positive Attitude

Wiese offers practical strategies for cultivating a positive attitude:

1. **Mindfulness and Gratitude:** Practicing mindfulness and gratitude can help individuals stay grounded and appreciate the present moment. Taking time to acknowledge

and express gratitude for achievements, opportunities, and supportive relationships reinforces a positive mindset.

2. **Visualization:** Visualization techniques involve mentally picturing success and achieving goals. By visualizing positive outcomes, individuals can boost confidence, clarify objectives, and maintain motivation during challenging times.

3. **Affirmations:** Affirmations are positive statements that individuals repeat to themselves regularly. These affirmations reinforce self-belief, challenge negative self-talk, and promote a constructive self-image.

4. **Surrounding Yourself with Positivity:** Surrounding oneself with supportive and optimistic individuals can significantly influence one's own mindset. Building a network of mentors, peers, and friends who embody positivity and encouragement creates a conducive environment for personal and professional growth.

5. **Continuous Learning and Adaptation:** Embracing a growth mindset involves viewing challenges as opportunities for learning and improvement. By continuously seeking new knowledge, acquiring new skills, and adapting to changing circumstances, individuals can maintain a resilient and positive outlook.

In Summary

In conclusion, cultivating a positive attitude is not just about maintaining optimism; it is about harnessing the transformative power of positivity to achieve personal and professional success. Christo Wiese's insights underscore the importance of focusing on what can go right, embracing positive thinking as a driver for achievement, and implementing practical strategies for maintaining a constructive mindset. By adopting a proactive and optimistic approach, individuals can overcome challenges, inspire others, and create a path towards fulfilling their goals and aspirations in business and beyond.

Chapter 9: The Biggest Misconception About Making Money

Opportunistic Nature of Business

No Universal Blueprint for Making Money

Christo Wiese challenges one of the most pervasive misconceptions about making money: the belief in a universal blueprint or formula for success in business. Throughout his extensive career in entrepreneurship and retail, Wiese has observed that **successful business ventures rarely follow a predetermined path or one-size-fits-all strategy.**

The idea of a blueprint suggests a linear, predictable approach to achieving financial success. It implies that there is a set formula or method that guarantees profitability and prosperity in any business endeavor. However, Wiese argues that this mindset overlooks the dynamic and unpredictable nature of the business landscape.

Business success, according to Wiese, is often the result of seizing opportunistic moments rather than adhering to a rigid plan. Entrepreneurs must be adaptable and agile, ready to capitalize on emerging trends, market shifts, and unforeseen opportunities. This opportunistic mindset requires flexibility, creativity, and a keen ability to recognize and act upon favorable conditions.

Business as a Series of Opportunistic Decisions

Instead of following a predefined blueprint, Wiese advocates for viewing business as a series of opportunistic decisions. **Successful entrepreneurs continuously assess and evaluate potential opportunities**, weighing risks and rewards before making strategic decisions. This proactive approach allows them to pivot and adjust their strategies based on changing market dynamics and consumer behaviors.

Wiese's own career trajectory exemplifies this opportunistic approach. From his early ventures in retail to his strategic expansions into diverse industries, Wiese made decisions based on real-time market insights and entrepreneurial intuition rather than rigid plans. His ability to identify and capitalize on emerging opportunities has been a key driver of his success.

Moreover, Wiese emphasizes the importance of remaining adaptable in the face of uncertainty. Economic conditions, technological advancements, and consumer preferences are constantly evolving, presenting new opportunities and challenges. Entrepreneurs who embrace an opportunistic mindset are better equipped to navigate these changes and position their businesses for sustained growth.

Practical Implications for Entrepreneurs

THE 17 BUSINESS LESSONS INSIGHTS FROM CHRISTO WIESE

For aspiring entrepreneurs and business leaders, understanding the opportunistic nature of business has several practical implications:

1. **Flexibility and Adaptability:** Developing a mindset that is open to change and responsive to opportunities allows entrepreneurs to stay ahead of competitors and capitalize on emerging trends.

2. **Risk Management:** Evaluating risks and rewards when making opportunistic decisions helps mitigate potential setbacks and enhances the likelihood of success.

3. **Innovation and Creativity:** Embracing an opportunistic approach encourages innovation and creativity, fostering a culture of experimentation and forward-thinking within organizations.

4. **Continuous Learning:** Remaining vigilant and staying informed about industry trends and market developments enables entrepreneurs to identify new opportunities for growth and expansion.

In Summary

In conclusion, Christo Wiese's insights challenge the misconception of a universal blueprint for making money in business. By recognizing the opportunistic nature of entrepreneurship and embracing a proactive approach to decision-making, entrepreneurs can position themselves for long-term success. Business success often hinges on the ability to seize opportunities, adapt to change, and innovate in response to evolving market conditions. By cultivating an opportunistic mindset, entrepreneurs can navigate the complexities of the business landscape and create sustainable value for their ventures.

Chapter 10: The Killer Mistake People Make When Starting Out

Staying Grounded

Dangers of Escalating Personal Lifestyle Prematurely
Christo Wiese identifies a common pitfall that many entrepreneurs encounter when starting out: the temptation to escalate their personal lifestyle prematurely upon achieving initial success. This mistake often manifests as a desire to flaunt newfound wealth through extravagant purchases, luxurious vacations, or upgrading to a lavish lifestyle.

Entrepreneurs may feel compelled to reward themselves for their hard work and accomplishments, and there is a natural inclination to enjoy the fruits of their labor. However, Wiese cautions that succumbing to this temptation too early can have detrimental effects on both personal finances and business sustainability.

The danger lies in diverting resources away from business growth and reinvestment. Entrepreneurial ventures require substantial capital, especially during the early stages of development. Every dollar diverted towards personal luxuries is a dollar that could potentially be invested back into the business to fuel expansion, innovation, and long-term profitability.

Moreover, escalating personal lifestyle prematurely can create financial strain and undermine financial stability. Entrepreneurs may find themselves living beyond their means, relying on unsustainable income streams, or accumulating debt to sustain an extravagant lifestyle. This financial pressure can distract from business priorities and hinder entrepreneurial success.

Keeping Passion and Focus on the Business

Another critical aspect of staying grounded is maintaining passion and focus on the business itself. **Entrepreneurship demands unwavering commitment**, dedication, and resilience. It requires entrepreneurs to prioritize the long-term vision and strategic objectives of their ventures over short-term gratification.

Wiese advocates for channeling passion and energy into building and scaling the business. This involves reinvesting profits into business operations, research and development, talent acquisition, and market expansion initiatives. By maintaining a steadfast focus on business growth and sustainability, entrepreneurs can position their ventures for long-term success and resilience in competitive markets.

Furthermore, keeping passion alive ensures that entrepreneurs remain engaged and motivated amidst challenges and setbacks. Entrepreneurship is a journey fraught with uncertainties, and maintaining a deep-seated passion for the industry, product, or service offering can provide the drive needed to overcome obstacles and persevere through difficult times.

Practical Strategies for Staying Grounded

Wiese offers practical strategies for entrepreneurs to stay grounded and focused on business priorities:

1. **Financial Discipline:** Implementing strict financial discipline and budgeting practices can help entrepreneurs manage personal and business finances responsibly. Separating personal and business expenses ensures that resources are allocated appropriately and prioritized for business growth.

2. **Long-Term Vision:** Continuously revisiting and reaffirming the long-term vision and strategic goals of the business reinforces commitment and focus. Aligning daily actions with overarching objectives helps entrepreneurs stay on track and avoid distractions that detract from business success.

3. **Seeking Mentorship and Guidance:** Engaging with experienced mentors, advisors, or peer networks can provide valuable perspective and guidance. Mentors can offer insights based on their own entrepreneurial journeys, helping entrepreneurs navigate challenges and make informed decisions.

4. **Celebrating Milestones Appropriately:** While it is important to acknowledge achievements and milestones, celebrating responsibly and within means ensures that celebrations do not overshadow business priorities. Maintaining humility and perspective reinforces a balanced approach to success and personal fulfillment.

In Summary

In In Summary, Christo Wiese underscores the importance of staying grounded when starting out in entrepreneurship. Avoiding the temptation to escalate personal lifestyle prematurely and maintaining passion and focus on the business are critical to long-term success. By prioritizing financial discipline, aligning actions with long-term vision, seeking mentorship, and celebrating milestones responsibly, entrepreneurs can cultivate a sustainable foundation for business growth and resilience. Staying grounded ensures that entrepreneurs remain committed to their entrepreneurial journey, navigate challenges effectively, and achieve sustainable success in competitive markets.

Chapter 11:
Combatting Your
Own Weaknesses

Self-Awareness

Acknowledging and Addressing Personal Weaknesses Christo Wiese emphasizes the importance of self-awareness in entrepreneurship, particularly in acknowledging and addressing personal weaknesses. **Self-awareness involves a deep understanding of one's strengths, limitations, and areas for improvement.** For entrepreneurs, this introspective ability is crucial for personal growth, effective leadership, and building successful ventures.

Acknowledging personal weaknesses is not a sign of weakness but a demonstration of humility and a commitment to continuous improvement. Entrepreneurs who recognize their limitations can take proactive steps to mitigate weaknesses and leverage strengths effectively. This self-awareness enables them to make informed decisions, seek appropriate support, and cultivate a balanced leadership approach.

Wiese encourages entrepreneurs to conduct regular self-assessments to identify areas where they may need development or additional resources. This introspective process involves reflecting on past experiences, seeking feedback from mentors or peers, and assessing performance against personal and professional goals. By identifying specific weaknesses, entrepreneurs can create targeted strategies for improvement and growth.

Importance of Support Systems and Team Reliance

In combating personal weaknesses, Wiese highlights the significance of support systems and team reliance. **Entrepreneurship is a collaborative endeavor that requires diverse skills, perspectives, and expertise.** Building a supportive team allows entrepreneurs to complement their strengths with the skills and talents of others, creating a robust foundation for business success.

Effective team reliance involves delegating responsibilities, leveraging team members' strengths, and fostering a culture of collaboration and accountability. Entrepreneurs who surround themselves with capable and motivated individuals can delegate tasks, streamline operations, and focus on strategic priorities. This collective effort enhances productivity, innovation, and resilience within the organization.

Moreover, support systems extend beyond the immediate team to include mentors, advisors, and professional networks. These external resources provide valuable guidance, feedback, and strategic insights that complement an entrepreneur's skill set. Engaging with mentors or participating in peer networks allows entrepreneurs to gain fresh perspectives, access industry knowledge, and navigate challenges with greater confidence.

Practical Strategies for Combatting Weaknesses

THE 17 BUSINESS LESSONS INSIGHTS FROM CHRISTO WIESE

Wiese offers practical strategies for entrepreneurs to combat personal weaknesses and leverage support systems effectively:

1. **Self-Development Plans:** Developing personalized self-development plans helps entrepreneurs address specific weaknesses and capitalize on strengths. Setting measurable goals, acquiring new skills through training or education, and seeking mentorship contribute to continuous improvement and professional growth.

2. **Building a Diverse Team:** Recruiting individuals with complementary skills and expertise enhances team dynamics and operational efficiency. Entrepreneurs should prioritize diversity in hiring to foster innovation, creativity, and adaptability within the organization.

3. **Creating a Culture of Feedback:** Establishing a culture of open communication and constructive feedback encourages team members to share insights, identify opportunities for improvement, and address challenges proactively. Regular performance reviews, peer evaluations, and team meetings promote transparency and accountability.

4. **Networking and Mentorship:** Actively engaging in professional networks, industry associations, and mentorship programs facilitates knowledge sharing, expands professional contacts, and provides access to valuable resources. Building meaningful relationships with mentors and peers fosters personal growth, career advancement, and business success.

In Summary

In conclusion, combatting personal weaknesses requires entrepreneurs to embrace self-awareness, acknowledge limitations, and leverage support systems effectively. By identifying areas for improvement, cultivating a diverse and capable team, and engaging with mentors and professional networks, entrepreneurs can strengthen their leadership capabilities and enhance organizational resilience. Self-awareness empowers entrepreneurs to navigate challenges with confidence, foster innovation, and achieve sustainable success in dynamic and competitive business environments.

Chapter 12: Timing and 'Lucky Breaks'

Positioning for Opportunity

B*eing Active and Engaged to Seize Opportunities*
Christo Wiese underscores the importance of proactive engagement and readiness to seize opportunities as they arise. In the area of entrepreneurship and business, timing often plays a pivotal role in determining success. Wiese advocates for a proactive approach, where entrepreneurs actively position themselves to capitalize on favorable market conditions, emerging trends, and serendipitous opportunities.

Being active involves staying informed about industry developments, economic trends, and market dynamics. Entrepreneurs who maintain a keen awareness of external factors are better equipped to identify potential opportunities and anticipate shifts in consumer behavior or industry trends. This proactive stance enables them to adapt quickly, pivot strategies, and capitalize on emerging opportunities before competitors.

Moreover, active engagement extends beyond passive observation to proactive networking and relationship-building. Networking allows entrepreneurs to expand their professional contacts, forge strategic partnerships, and cultivate valuable relationships within their industry. By nurturing a diverse network of contacts, entrepreneurs increase their visibility, access new opportunities, and gain insights from peers and industry experts.

The Role of Staying Informed and Networking

Staying informed is a cornerstone of effective opportunity positioning. Entrepreneurs must prioritize continuous learning, staying updated on industry trends, technological advancements, and regulatory changes that may impact their business. This knowledge empowers entrepreneurs to make informed decisions, anticipate challenges, and identify opportunities for innovation and growth.

Networking plays a complementary role in opportunity positioning by facilitating knowledge sharing, collaboration, and access to resources. Engaging in professional associations, industry conferences, and networking events allows entrepreneurs to exchange ideas, gain industry insights, and discover potential collaborators or investors. Building meaningful relationships through networking opens doors to new opportunities, partnerships, and business ventures.

Practical Strategies for Positioning for Opportunity

Wiese offers practical strategies for entrepreneurs to effectively position themselves for opportunity:

1. **Continuous Learning:** Committing to lifelong learning through reading industry publications, attending seminars, and participating in webinars ensures entrepreneurs remain informed and adaptable to changing market conditions.

2. **Networking and Relationship-Building:** Actively participating in networking events, joining professional

associations, and leveraging social media platforms enhances visibility and expands professional connections. Building genuine relationships fosters collaboration, knowledge exchange, and potential business opportunities.

3. **Market Research and Analysis:** Conducting thorough market research and competitive analysis provides insights into consumer preferences, market trends, and emerging opportunities. This information enables entrepreneurs to identify underserved markets, anticipate demand shifts, and develop targeted strategies to capitalize on market opportunities.

4. **Adaptability and Agility:** Maintaining a flexible and agile approach allows entrepreneurs to pivot quickly in response to changing market dynamics or unexpected opportunities. Embracing innovation, experimenting with new ideas, and embracing calculated risks position entrepreneurs to seize opportunities and drive business growth.

In Summary

In conclusion, timing and 'lucky breaks' in business are often the result of proactive engagement, strategic positioning, and continuous readiness to seize opportunities. By staying informed, actively engaging in networking, and maintaining agility, entrepreneurs can enhance their ability to capitalize on favorable market conditions and navigate challenges effectively. Positioning for opportunity requires a combination of foresight, adaptability, and a proactive mindset, enabling entrepreneurs to achieve sustainable success and drive innovation in competitive business environments.

Chapter 13: Being Born on 'The Back Foot'

Defining Your Own Fate

O*vercoming Societal Limitations and Prejudices*
Christo Wiese delves into the concept of being born on 'the back foot,' addressing societal limitations and prejudices that individuals may face based on factors such as socioeconomic background, ethnicity, gender, or educational opportunities. Despite these challenges, Wiese emphasizes the importance of resilience, determination, and self-belief in overcoming adversity and defining one's own fate.

Societal limitations can manifest as stereotypes, biases, or systemic barriers that restrict opportunities for certain individuals or groups. These limitations may create obstacles in accessing education, employment, or entrepreneurial opportunities, thereby perpetuating cycles of inequality and disadvantage. Wiese challenges readers to confront and transcend these limitations through perseverance and a steadfast commitment to personal growth and achievement.

Belief in Self-Determination and Personal Potential

Central to Wiese's philosophy is the belief in self-determination and the inherent potential of every individual to shape their own destiny. He encourages readers to reject fatalistic attitudes and embrace a mindset of empowerment, recognizing that personal agency and initiative are pivotal in achieving success and fulfillment.

Self-determination entails taking ownership of one's decisions, actions, and outcomes, regardless of external circumstances or past experiences. It involves setting ambitious goals, cultivating resilience in the face of setbacks, and pursuing opportunities that align with personal values and aspirations. Wiese's own journey from humble beginnings to entrepreneurial success serves as a testimony to the transformative power of self-belief and perseverance.

Practical Strategies for Defining Your Own Fate

Wiese offers practical strategies for individuals to define their own fate and overcome societal limitations:

1. **Self-Reflection and Goal Setting:** Engaging in self-reflection allows individuals to identify personal strengths, weaknesses, and aspirations. Setting clear, achievable goals provides direction and motivation for pursuing meaningful endeavors despite challenges or setbacks.

2. **Education and Skill Development:** Investing in education, skill development, and continuous learning enhances personal competence and opens doors to new opportunities. Lifelong learning equips individuals with the knowledge, skills, and confidence needed to navigate complex environments and achieve professional growth.

3. **Resilience and Adaptability:** Cultivating resilience enables individuals to bounce back from adversity, learn from

setbacks, and persevere in pursuit of long-term goals. Embracing adaptability allows for flexibility in responding to changing circumstances and seizing unexpected opportunities for personal and professional advancement.

4. **Advocacy and Community Engagement:** Advocating for social justice, equity, and inclusion fosters positive change within communities and promotes equal access to opportunities for all individuals. Engaging in community initiatives, mentorship programs, or advocacy efforts empowers individuals to contribute to collective efforts in dismantling systemic barriers and promoting fairness.

In Summary

In conclusion, being born on 'the back foot' necessitates overcoming societal limitations and embracing self-determination to define one's own fate. By challenging stereotypes, cultivating resilience, and advocating for equity, individuals can transcend barriers and achieve personal fulfillment and success. Wiese's insights underscore the transformative potential of resilience, determination, and a proactive mindset in overcoming adversity and shaping a brighter future. Ultimately, defining one's own fate requires a steadfast commitment to personal growth, empowerment, and the pursuit of meaningful opportunities in pursuit of a more equitable and inclusive society.

Chapter 14: The Most Basic Principle of Managing Money

Inflow and Outflow

M*anaging Money Like a Dam*
Christo Wiese introduces a fundamental principle of financial management likened to managing a dam. Just as a dam controls the flow of water, effective money management involves regulating both the **inflow (income)** and **outflow (expenses)** of financial resources. This analogy emphasizes the importance of maintaining balance and stability in personal or business finances to achieve long-term financial security and sustainability.

Limiting Outflow and Maximizing Inflow

Central to Wiese's approach is the concept of limiting outflow and maximizing inflow. This dual strategy focuses on optimizing financial resources by:

1. **Limiting Outflow:** Controlling expenditures and expenses is crucial to preserving financial capital and ensuring that money is allocated efficiently. This involves adopting prudent spending habits, prioritizing needs over wants, and

avoiding unnecessary or extravagant purchases that can deplete financial resources unnecessarily.

2. **Maximizing Inflow:** Increasing income streams and revenue sources enhances financial liquidity and resilience. Entrepreneurs and individuals can achieve this by diversifying income sources, pursuing new business opportunities, investing in income-generating assets, or enhancing professional skills to command higher earnings potential.

Practical Strategies for Managing Money Effectively

Wiese provides practical strategies for implementing the principles of managing money like a dam:

1. **Budgeting and Financial Planning:** Developing a comprehensive budget and financial plan enables individuals and businesses to track income and expenses, allocate resources effectively, and prioritize financial goals. Regularly reviewing and adjusting budgets ensures financial discipline and accountability.

2. **Expense Management:** Adopting frugal spending habits, negotiating favorable terms with suppliers or service providers, and eliminating unnecessary expenses contribute to reducing outflow and preserving financial capital. Implementing cost-saving measures and budgetary controls supports long-term financial stability.

3. **Income Generation:** Exploring diverse income streams, leveraging market opportunities, and investing in income-generating assets (e.g., stocks, bonds, real estate) diversifies revenue sources and enhances financial resilience. Developing additional skills or pursuing entrepreneurial ventures can supplement primary income and create financial security.

4. **Risk Management:** Mitigating financial risks through insurance coverage, emergency savings funds, and prudent investment strategies safeguards against unexpected expenses or income disruptions. Establishing contingency plans and maintaining liquidity prepares individuals and businesses to navigate economic uncertainties effectively.

In Summary

In conclusion, managing money like a dam involves balancing inflow and outflow to achieve financial stability and prosperity. By controlling expenses, maximizing income opportunities, and implementing sound financial practices, individuals and businesses can build resilience, achieve financial goals, and sustain long-term wealth accumulation. Christo Wiese's principle underscores the importance of disciplined financial management, strategic planning, and proactive decision-making in securing financial well-being and pursuing financial independence.

Chapter 15:
Compound Interest

Understanding Compound Interest

Compound interest is a powerful financial concept that can work either to an individual's advantage or disadvantage, depending on whether it applies to investments or debt. Christo Wiese emphasizes the significance of understanding and leveraging compound interest to achieve financial growth and stability.

Benefits of Compound Interest for Investments

When it comes to investments, compound interest can significantly amplify wealth over time. The core principle of compound interest is that it allows the interest earned on an investment to be reinvested, generating additional interest. This cycle of earning interest on both the initial principal and the accumulated interest leads to exponential growth.

1. **Growth Over Time:** The longer the investment period, the more pronounced the effects of compound interest. For example, even modest contributions to a retirement fund can grow substantially over several decades due to the compounding effect.

2. **Reinvestment:** Regularly reinvesting dividends or interest payments ensures that the investment continues to grow at an accelerating rate. This reinvestment strategy is crucial for maximizing the benefits of compound interest.

3. **High-Yield Investments:** Selecting investments with higher interest rates or returns can further enhance the compounding effect. Stocks, bonds, mutual funds, and real estate are examples of assets that can benefit from compound interest.

Detriments of Compound Interest for Debt

Conversely, compound interest can be detrimental when applied to debt. In the case of loans or credit card debt, the interest charges accumulate on both the principal and the previously accrued interest, leading to a rapid increase in the total amount owed.

1. **Escalating Debt:** Without prompt repayments, the compounding interest on debt can cause the balance to grow quickly, making it challenging to pay off the debt. This is especially true for high-interest debts such as credit card balances.

2. **Minimum Payments:** Paying only the minimum amount due on loans or credit cards often results in prolonged repayment periods and significantly higher total interest costs. The compounding interest continues to increase the debt burden.

3. **Financial Strain:** Compound interest on debt can create a cycle of financial strain, where individuals find it increasingly difficult to manage their finances and allocate funds towards other essential expenses or savings.

*Practical Strategies for Leveraging and Managing
Compound Interest*

To harness the benefits of compound interest for investments and mitigate its negative impact on debt, Wiese offers practical strategies:

1. **Early and Consistent Investing:** Starting to invest early in life and making regular contributions to investment accounts maximizes the compounding effect. Even small, consistent investments can grow substantially over time.

2. **Debt Repayment:** Prioritizing the repayment of high-interest debts and avoiding accruing additional debt are critical steps in managing compound interest. Paying more than the minimum amount due can significantly reduce the total interest paid and shorten the repayment period.

3. **Savings and Retirement Accounts:** Utilizing tax-advantaged savings and retirement accounts, can enhance the benefits of compound interest. These accounts often offer compounding returns along with tax benefits.

4. **Financial Discipline:** Maintaining financial discipline by living within one's means, budgeting effectively, and avoiding unnecessary debt can help individuals leverage compound interest for wealth accumulation rather than falling victim to its detrimental effects on debt.

In Summary

In conclusion, compound interest is a double-edged sword that can either propel financial growth through investments or exacerbate financial burdens through debt. By understanding and strategically leveraging the power of compound interest, individuals can achieve significant long-term financial benefits. Conversely, managing and minimizing compound interest on debt is essential for maintaining financial health and stability. Christo Wiese's insights highlight the critical role of compound interest in personal and business finance, emphasizing the need for informed financial decision-making and disciplined financial practices.

Chapter 16:
Managing Debt

Balanced Approach to Debt

Debt is often viewed negatively, but Christo Wiese advocates for a more balanced perspective, emphasizing that **debt can be a valuable tool when managed properly**. Understanding how to leverage debt responsibly and ensuring protection against debt-related risks are key components of effective financial management.

Debt as a Tool, Not an Evil

Debt, when used strategically, can enable growth and opportunity. It provides access to capital that might not be readily available, allowing individuals and businesses to invest in opportunities that can generate significant returns.

1. **Leveraging Debt for Growth:** Businesses often use debt to finance expansion, invest in new projects, or purchase assets that can enhance productivity and profitability. For individuals, debt can be used to buy a home, fund education, or invest in ventures that promise future gains.

2. **Cost of Capital:** Debt can sometimes be cheaper than equity, especially in environments with low-interest rates. By

borrowing, businesses can retain ownership and control while still accessing the funds needed for growth.

3. **Tax Benefits:** Interest payments on debt are often tax-deductible, which can reduce the overall cost of borrowing. This tax advantage makes debt an attractive option for financing certain expenditures.

Ensuring Adequate Protection Against Debt-Related Risks

While debt can be a useful tool, it carries risks that need to be managed carefully. The potential for financial strain increases if debt levels become unmanageable or if external conditions change unfavorably.

1. **Creating a Buffer:** Having a financial buffer or reserve is essential to manage unforeseen circumstances such as economic downturns, currency fluctuations, or changes in interest rates. This buffer can prevent a liquidity crisis and provide time to adjust to new conditions.

2. **Diversifying Income Streams:** Relying on multiple income sources can mitigate the risk associated with debt. For businesses, this means diversifying revenue streams to avoid over-reliance on a single product or market. For individuals, it could mean having multiple streams of income to ensure stability.

3. **Interest Rate Management:** Keeping an eye on interest rates and choosing fixed rates over variable rates can provide more predictable debt servicing costs. This helps in planning and budgeting more effectively.

4. **Debt-to-Equity Ratio:** Maintaining a healthy balance between debt and equity ensures that the business or individual does not become over-leveraged. A high debt-to-equity ratio

can increase financial risk, so it is essential to monitor and manage this ratio.

5. **Regular Financial Reviews:** Conducting regular reviews of financial health helps in identifying potential issues early. This includes assessing cash flow, reviewing debt obligations, and making adjustments as necessary to maintain financial stability.

Practical Strategies for Managing Debt

1. **Prudent Borrowing:** Only borrow what is necessary and ensure that the borrowed funds are used for productive purposes that can generate returns exceeding the cost of the debt.

2. **Debt Repayment Plans:** Establish clear repayment plans and prioritize paying off high-interest debt first. This reduces the overall interest burden and accelerates the journey to being debt-free.

3. **Refinancing Options:** Explore refinancing options to take advantage of lower interest rates or better terms. Refinancing can reduce monthly payments and make debt more manageable.

4. **Avoiding Unnecessary Debt:** Be cautious about taking on debt for non-essential purposes. Unnecessary debt can lead to financial strain and limit flexibility in managing finances.

In Summary

In conclusion, managing debt effectively involves viewing it as a strategic tool rather than an inherent evil. By leveraging debt wisely and ensuring adequate protection against potential risks, individuals and businesses can achieve growth and financial stability.

Christo Wiese's insights into debt management highlight the importance of a balanced approach, emphasizing the need for careful planning, prudent borrowing, and regular financial reviews. Through disciplined debt management, it is possible to harness the benefits of debt while minimizing its risks, ultimately contributing to long-term financial success and resilience.

Chapter 17: Being a Great Leader

Leadership Qualities

Christo Wiese's perspective on leadership encompasses a blend of inspiration, hard work, strategic planning, and emotional intelligence. **True leadership goes beyond mere management; it involves motivating and guiding people to achieve extraordinary results.** Here are the key qualities that define great leadership according to Wiese:

Inspiring People and Working Hard

A great leader inspires others to reach their full potential. This inspiration stems from the leader's own dedication and hard work, which sets a powerful example for the team to follow.

1. **Motivation:** A leader must be able to articulate a compelling vision that excites and motivates people. This involves communicating the purpose and goals of the organization in a way that resonates with the team and makes them feel part of something greater than themselves.

2. **Dedication:** Hard work and commitment from the leader set a standard for the rest of the team. When a leader is

seen working diligently and passionately, it encourages others to match that effort and dedication.

Clear Planning and Leading by Example

Effective leadership involves strategic planning and demonstrating the behaviors and attitudes that leaders wish to see in their team members.

1. **Strategic Vision:** A clear plan is essential for guiding an organization towards its goals. This includes setting long-term objectives, developing actionable steps, and regularly reviewing progress to ensure the team stays on track.

2. **Leading by Example:** Leaders must embody the values and work ethic they expect from their team. By consistently demonstrating integrity, accountability, and perseverance, leaders can foster a culture of excellence and mutual respect.

Balancing Intelligence with Humility

While intelligence is important, **humility is equally critical for effective leadership.** Leaders must recognize that they do not have all the answers and be open to learning from others.

1. **Intellectual Humility:** Acknowledging the limits of one's knowledge and seeking input from others fosters a collaborative environment. It also encourages team members to share their ideas and expertise, leading to better decision-making and innovation.

2. **Avoiding Arrogance:** Humility prevents leaders from becoming arrogant and disconnected from their team. By remaining approachable and respectful, leaders can build strong, trusting relationships with their team members.

Importance of Emotional Quotient (EQ) over Intelligence Quotient (IQ)

Emotional intelligence (EQ) is the ability to understand and manage one's own emotions, as well as the emotions of others. Wiese emphasizes that EQ is more important than IQ in leadership.

1. **Self-Awareness:** Leaders with high EQ are aware of their own emotional states and how these can affect their behavior and decision-making. This self-awareness helps them remain composed and effective under pressure.

2. **Empathy:** Understanding and empathizing with the emotions of team members is crucial for building strong interpersonal relationships. Leaders with high EQ can better address the needs and concerns of their team, fostering a supportive and productive work environment.

3. **Effective Communication:** High EQ enhances communication skills. Leaders who can express themselves clearly and listen actively can resolve conflicts, provide constructive feedback, and build consensus more effectively.

4. **Adaptability:** Emotional intelligence enables leaders to adapt their management style to different situations and individuals. This flexibility is essential for navigating the complexities of leadership and responding to changing circumstances.

In Summary

In conclusion, being a great leader involves a combination of inspiration, hard work, strategic planning, and emotional intelligence. By motivating and inspiring their team, leading by example, balancing intelligence with humility, and prioritizing emotional intelligence, leaders can create an environment where people feel valued, motivated, and capable of achieving extraordinary results. Christo Wiese's insights into leadership highlight the importance of these qualities in fostering a positive and productive organizational culture, ultimately driving long-term success and fulfillment for both leaders and their teams.

Chapter 18: The Single Most Important Characteristic You Need to Succeed in Business

Incurable Optimism

Christo Wiese emphasizes that **the single most important characteristic for success in business is incurable optimism.** This trait involves a steadfast belief in positive outcomes and an unwavering focus on possibilities rather than obstacles. Embracing optimism can transform how entrepreneurs approach challenges, fueling persistence and driving long-term success.

Embracing Positivity and Seeing Life Optimistically

Optimism is more than just a positive outlook; it's a mindset that influences every aspect of an entrepreneur's journey.

1. **Positive Outlook:** Optimistic individuals focus on the potential for success rather than the fear of failure. They see challenges as opportunities for growth and learning rather than

insurmountable obstacles. This positive outlook helps maintain motivation and enthusiasm even in the face of difficulties.

2. **Resilience:** Optimism breeds resilience. When setbacks occur, optimistic entrepreneurs are more likely to bounce back and continue pursuing their goals. They view failures as temporary and believe in their ability to overcome them, which is crucial for long-term success.

3. **Proactive Attitude:** Optimists take proactive steps to shape their future. Instead of waiting for things to improve, they actively seek solutions and take initiatives to create positive change. This proactive approach can lead to innovative ideas and new opportunities.

How Optimism Fuels Persistence and Success

Optimism plays a critical role in sustaining the persistence needed to achieve success in business.

1. **Sustained Motivation:** Optimism keeps entrepreneurs motivated, even during tough times. When faced with challenges, an optimistic mindset encourages them to keep pushing forward and maintain their efforts, knowing that perseverance will eventually lead to success.

2. **Overcoming Obstacles:** An optimistic attitude helps entrepreneurs view obstacles as temporary setbacks rather than permanent barriers. This perspective allows them to remain focused on their goals and find creative solutions to problems that arise.

3. **Attracting Opportunities:** Optimistic people are more likely to attract opportunities and build strong networks. Their positive energy and outlook make them more approachable and trustworthy, leading to fruitful collaborations and partnerships.

4. **Encouraging Team Spirit:** Optimism isn't just beneficial for the individual; it also positively impacts the entire team. A leader's optimistic attitude can inspire and uplift their team, creating a work environment where everyone feels motivated and valued. This collective positivity can enhance productivity and drive the organization towards its goals.

5. **Long-Term Vision:** Optimists tend to have a long-term vision and are more patient in working towards their goals. They understand that success doesn't come overnight and are willing to put in the necessary time and effort to achieve their aspirations. This long-term perspective helps them stay committed and focused, even when immediate results are not evident.

Strategies to Cultivate Incurable Optimism

1. **Positive Self-Talk:** Replace negative thoughts with positive affirmations. Encourage yourself with optimistic statements that reinforce your belief in your abilities and potential for success.

2. **Surround Yourself with Positivity:** Engage with people who uplift and inspire you. Avoid negative influences that can dampen your optimism. Build a supportive network of mentors, peers, and friends who share a positive outlook.

3. **Focus on Solutions:** Instead of dwelling on problems, direct your energy towards finding solutions. This problem-solving approach keeps you proactive and prevents you from feeling overwhelmed by challenges.

4. **Celebrate Small Wins:** Acknowledge and celebrate your achievements, no matter how small. Recognizing progress boosts your confidence and reinforces your optimistic outlook.

5. **Learn from Setbacks:** View failures as learning experiences. Analyze what went wrong, extract valuable lessons, and use that knowledge to improve and move forward with renewed optimism.

In Summary

In conclusion incurable optimism is a cornerstone of success in business. By embracing a positive outlook, entrepreneurs can maintain motivation, overcome obstacles, and attract opportunities that lead to long-term success. Optimism fuels persistence, encourages innovative thinking, and creates a positive work environment that benefits both the individual and the team. Christo Wiese's insights underscore the importance of cultivating and maintaining optimism as a vital characteristic for anyone seeking to thrive in the dynamic world of business.

In AS Wrap Up

Recap of Lessons

THROUGHOUT THIS BOOK, we have explored the 17 invaluable business lessons shared by South African retail magnate **Christo Wiese**. These lessons, drawn from his decades of experience and success, offer profound insights into what it takes to thrive in the business world. Let's summarize these lessons:

1. **The Biggest Business Lesson**: Success in business is accessible to anyone. Developing a philosophical framework based on faith, positivity, hard work, enthusiasm, and compassion is crucial.

2. **What You Need to Accept**: Business has its ups and downs. True success is measured by how you handle setbacks. Counting your blessings and never giving up are vital.

3. **Interpersonal Skills**: Treating people with respect and dignity, working well with others, and avoiding burning bridges are essential for long-term success.

4. **Making Difficult Decisions**: Embrace uncertainty. Approach decisions logically and decisively, and be adaptable to change.

5. **Why You Need to Be a Little Bit Crazy to Succeed**: Embrace the entrepreneurial spirit by maintaining motivation despite potential setbacks and uncertainties.

6. **Attaining vs Maintaining Wealth**: Making money is easier than keeping it. Stay vigilant, humble, and avoid believing in your own fairytale.

7. **The One Personality Flaw You Must Overcome**: Maintaining a positive attitude and focusing on what can go right drives achievement and success.

8. **The Biggest Misconception About Making Money**: There is no universal blueprint for making money. Business is opportunistic and involves assessing and seizing opportunities as they arise.

9. **The Killer Mistake People Make When Starting Out**: Stay grounded and avoid escalating your personal lifestyle prematurely. Focus on your passion and the core aspects of your business.

10. **Combatting Your Own Weaknesses**: Acknowledge and address personal weaknesses. Rely on support systems and team collaboration for success.

11. **Timing and 'Lucky Breaks'**: Be active and engaged to seize opportunities. Stay informed and network to position yourself for success.

12. **Being Born on 'The Back Foot'**: Overcome societal limitations and prejudices. Believe in self-determination and your potential to succeed.

13. ****The Most Basic Principle of Managing Money****: Manage money like a dam by limiting outflow and maximizing inflow.

14. **Compound Interest**: Understand the benefits of compound interest for investments and the detriments of compound interest for debt.

15. **Managing Debt**: View debt as a tool, not an evil. Ensure you have adequate protection against debt-related risks.

16. **Being a Great Leader**: Inspire people and work hard. Have a clear plan, lead by example, balance intelligence with

humility, and prioritize emotional intelligence (EQ) over intellectual intelligence (IQ).

17. The Single Most Important Characteristic You Need to Succeed in Business: Incurable optimism is key. Embrace positivity, see life optimistically, and let optimism fuel persistence and success.

Final Thoughts on Applying These Lessons in One's Own Business Journey

These 17 lessons from Christo Wiese provide a comprehensive roadmap for anyone looking to achieve success in business. However, it's not enough to simply understand these principles; you must actively apply them in your own entrepreneurial journey. Here are some final thoughts on how to integrate these lessons into your daily business practices:

1. **Reflect and Internalize**: Regularly reflect on these lessons and internalize them. Make them a part of your personal and professional philosophy.

2. **Stay Grounded and Humble**: No matter how successful you become, always stay grounded and humble. Remember that the journey is just as important as the destination.

3. **Build and Nurture Relationships**: Invest time and effort in building and nurturing relationships. Treat people with respect and dignity, and always be mindful of the long-term value of maintaining good relationships.

4. **Embrace Change and Adaptability**: The business landscape is constantly evolving. Embrace change and be adaptable. Stay informed, be proactive, and be ready to pivot when necessary.

5. **Maintain a Positive Attitude**: Cultivate a positive attitude. Focus on opportunities rather than obstacles. Let your optimism drive you forward, even in challenging times.

6. **Lead with Integrity and Empathy**: Strive to be a leader who inspires others. Lead with integrity, empathy, and humility. Balance your intelligence with emotional intelligence to create a supportive and productive work environment.

7. **Be Persistent and Resilient**: Success rarely comes without setbacks. Be persistent and resilient. Learn from your failures, and never give up on your dreams.

8. **Continuously Learn and Grow**: The most successful entrepreneurs are lifelong learners. Continuously seek out new knowledge, experiences, and perspectives to grow both personally and professionally.

9. **Stay Passionate and Committed**: Keep your passion and commitment to your business alive. Let your enthusiasm and dedication inspire others and drive your business towards success.

By applying these lessons and embodying the principles shared by Christo Wiese, you can navigate the complexities of the business world and build a successful and fulfilling entrepreneurial career. Remember, the journey to success is a marathon, not a sprint. Stay focused, stay positive, and keep moving forward.

Appendix

Resources

Recommended Readings on Entrepreneurship
1. "The Lean Startup" by Eric Ries

This book provides a scientific approach to creating and managing successful startups in an age when companies need to innovate more than ever.

2. "Zero to One: Notes on Startups, or How to Build the Future" by Peter Thiel

Peter Thiel, co-founder of PayPal, offers insights on how to build a successful startup that creates new things rather than improving existing products.

3. "The E-Myth Revisited: Why Most Small Businesses Don't Work and What to Do About It" by Michael E. Gerber

This classic book dispels the myths surrounding starting your own business and shows how commonplace assumptions can get in the way of running a successful business.

4. "Good to Great: Why Some Companies Make the Leap and Others Don't" by Jim Collins

Jim Collins explores why some companies make the transition from good to great and others don't. The book provides practical guidance for building a great company.

5. "Start with Why: How Great Leaders Inspire Everyone to Take Action" by Simon Sinek

Simon Sinek explains how leaders can inspire cooperation, trust, and change by starting with a clear sense of why they do what they do.

6. "The Innovator's Dilemma: When New Technologies Cause Great Firms to Fail" by Clayton M. Christensen

This book provides a set of rules that companies can use to avoid the pitfalls of disruptive innovation.

7. "The Hard Thing About Hard Things: Building a Business When There Are No Easy Answers" by Ben Horowitz

Ben Horowitz offers essential advice on building and running a startup—practical wisdom for managing the toughest problems business schools don't cover.

8. "Think and Grow Rich" by Napoleon Hill

This classic book is based on Hill's study of the habits of wealthy individuals. It provides timeless principles for achieving financial and personal success.

9. "The Art of the Start 2.0: The Time-Tested, Battle-Hardened Guide for Anyone Starting Anything" by Guy Kawasaki

Guy Kawasaki's book is a practical guide for anyone starting a new venture, packed with advice on everything from raising money to building a brand.

10. "Blue Ocean Strategy: How to Create Uncontested Market Space and Make the Competition Irrelevant" by W. Chan Kim and Renée Mauborgne

This book challenges everything you thought you knew about the requirements for strategic success. It provides a systematic approach to making the competition irrelevant.

Online Resources and Websites

1.   HARVARD   BUSINESS   Review   (HBR): hbr.org

A leading resource for business and management insights, offering articles, case studies, and research on a wide range of topics relevant to entrepreneurs.

2.   Entrepreneur   Magazine: [entrepreneur.com](https://www.entrepreneur.com)

A comprehensive resource for entrepreneurship, providing articles, guides, and advice on starting and running a business.

3.   TED   Talks   on   Entrepreneurship: [ted.com](https://www.ted.com/topics/entrepreneurship)

A collection of inspiring and informative talks by successful entrepreneurs and business leaders.

4.   Startup   Grind: [startupgrind.com](https://www.startupgrind.com)

A global community of entrepreneurs offering events, mentorship, and networking opportunities.

5. SCORE: [score.org](https://www.score.org)

A nonprofit organization that provides free mentoring and educational resources to small business owners.

6. **Y Combinator's Library**: [ycombinator.com/library](https://www.ycombinator.com/library)

A collection of essays, videos, and guides on startup advice from the world-renowned startup accelerator, Y Combinator.

7. **Coursera and edX**: [coursera.org](https://www.coursera.org) and [edx.org](https://www.edx.org)

These platforms offer courses on entrepreneurship and business management from top universities around the world.

Contact Information

FOR FURTHER ENGAGEMENT or inquiries, you can reach out through the following channels:

1. **Email**: davenjogu@bcreativefirm.co.ke

For questions, feedback, or additional information, feel free to send an email.

2. **Website:** [Babazuri Creative Firm](http://www.[1]bcreativefirm.co.ke[2])

Visit our website for more resources, updates, and information on upcoming events and publications.

3. **Social Media**

- **Twitter:** @bcreativefirm (https://[3]x[4].com/[5]bcreativefirm[6])

---

1. http://www.bcreativefirm.co.ke/

2. http://www.bcreativefirm.co.ke/

3. https://x.com/bcreativefirm

4. https://x.com/bcreativefirm

5. https://x.com/bcreativefirm

6. https://x.com/bcreativefirm

Connect with us for professional networking and opportunities.

- **Facebook:** @bcreativefirm (https://www.facebook.com/[7]bcreativefirm[8])

Join our community for discussions, resources, and support.

We look forward to engaging with you and supporting your entrepreneurial journey.

---

7. https://www.facebook.com/bcreativefirm

8. https://www.facebook.com/bcreativefirm

Don't miss out!

Visit the website below and you can sign up to receive emails whenever Dave Njogu publishes a new book. There's no charge and no obligation.

https://books2read.com/r/B-A-IGXZ-DVARD

BOOKS 2 READ

Connecting independent readers to independent writers.

Did you love *THE 17 BUSINESS LESSONS Insights from Christo Wiese*? Then you should read *The Quantity Advantage: Achieving Excellence Through Abundance*[9] by Dave Njogu!

[10]

Unlock the secrets to unparalleled success and mastery with **"The Quantity Advantage : Achieving Excellence Through Abundance."** This groundbreaking book shatters the myth of perfection, *revealing why producing more leads to better skills, improved habits, and extraordinary results.*

Are you tired of striving for perfection and getting nowhere? Do you find yourself procrastinating, endlessly planning, but never truly achieving your goals? It's time to

---

9. https://books2read.com/u/4Drg6g

10. https://books2read.com/u/4Drg6g

embrace a transformative approach that prioritizes action and consistent effort over the futile chase for flawlessness.

In "The Quantity Advantage," you will discover:

- **The Power of Practice:** Learn why making one hundred pots in a month trumps obsessing over a single perfect one. Real-world examples and compelling stories illustrate how quantity breeds excellence.

- **Action Over Procrastination:** Uncover practical strategies to stop procrastinating and start taking meaningful action today. Become the action-oriented person you've always wanted to be.

- **The AI Edge:** Harness the power of artificial intelligence to work smarter and faster. Stay ahead of the competition with cutting-edge tools and technologies that amplify your productivity and creativity.

- **Ultimate Productivity:** Master the art of the 3-4 hour workday. Discover time management techniques and prioritization methods that maximize your efficiency, allowing you to achieve more in less time.

- **Digital Entrepreneurship:** Explore the limitless opportunities in the digital economy. Learn how to build an online presence, monetize your skills, and become your own boss through digital writing, micro-education, and YouTube content creation.

- **Continuous Learning:** Embrace the importance of self-education and lifelong learning. Gain quick, impactful skills through micro-education and stay relevant in a rapidly changing world.

- **Optimal Health for Peak Performance:** Enhance your brain function and overall well-being with a nutritious diet rich in herbs, vegetables, and fruits. Discover relaxation techniques that reduce stress and boost mental clarity.

- **Habit Formation:** Develop and sustain habits that support your goals. Learn how consistency over perfection can lead to lasting success and personal growth.

"The Quantity Advantage : Achieving Excellence Through Abundance" is not just a book; it's a call to action. It's your guide to breaking free from the shackles of perfectionism and stepping into a world where doing more leads to becoming more. Whether you're an aspiring entrepreneur, a creative professional, or anyone seeking to improve their skills and habits, this book offers the blueprint for achieving mastery and living a more productive, fulfilling life.

Take the first step towards a future of limitless potential. Embrace the power of quantity, transform your habits, and become the master of your craft. Thank you for getting your copy of "The Quantity Advantage : Achieving Excellence Through Abundance" today your journey to excellence begins!

Read more at https://bcreativefirm.co.ke.

Also by Dave Njogu

101 Common Questions Answered
Mastering Business English Q&A

Standalone
The Healing Harvest: Organic Farming 101
Unlock Your Authorial Potential: The Ultimate Guide to Crafting and Selling eBooks Using ChatGPT and Draft2digit
Herbs and Spices: Nature's Remedies for Health and Wellness
Grit and Growth: Unleashing Mental Toughness for Small Business Success
Design Mastery: Principles of Page Layout and Typography for Beginners
The Quantity Advantage: Achieving Excellence Through Abundance
THE 17 BUSINESS LESSONS Insights from Christo Wiese

About the Author

I'm Dave Njogu. My authorship emanates from a deep-seated passion for continuous self-education. I utilize a potent blend of human ingenuity and AI to create transformative books aimed at inspiring productivity and resourcefulness.

Read more at https://bcreativefirm.co.ke.

About the Publisher

Babazuri Creative Firm originates from Kenya and operates as a Creative Agency primarily catering to small businesses.

Our expertise encompasses graphic design, the development of practical websites, video production, and more.

Additionally, we actively champion Linux and open-source software.